Genre Narrative Nonfiction

Essential Question
What can people accomplish by working together?

COMING TOGETHER FOR CHANGE

BY VICTORIA TREMPER

INTRODUCTION

Every day, people around the world work to make their communities stronger.

Many good ideas begin with one person working in **solitude**. Next, that person shares his or her idea with others. The other people then add ideas of their own. Then more people want to join in and get **involved**.

By working together, people can learn from one another. They can achieve more than they ever thought possible.

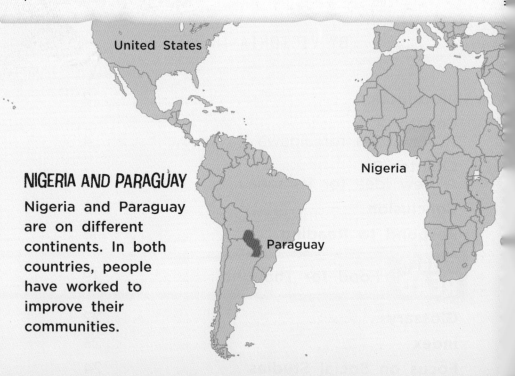

United States

Nigeria

Paraguay

NIGERIA AND PARAGUAY

Nigeria and Paraguay are on different continents. In both countries, people have worked to improve their communities.

People in Nigeria and Paraguay have used their **ingenuity** to solve **local** problems. They improved life for the people in their communities.

More people in Nigeria live in rural areas than in cities.

In each country, someone came up with a creative idea. Each idea used local talent and resources. One person is a teacher from Nigeria. He grew up in a **rural**, or country, area. The other grew up in a city in Paraguay. Even though they come from different backgrounds, they have something important in common. They both worked with others to improve people's lives.

CHAPTER 1
A NEW IDEA FOR JIGAWA

Nigeria has many modern towns. It also has rural areas that don't have **refrigeration**. Jigawa is an **impoverished** rural area in Nigeria. Many homes there do not have electricity. That means there are no lights, no television, and no refrigeration.

The lack of refrigeration makes life difficult for people in Jigawa. Many people there are **subsistence** farmers. They grow only enough food for their families, and there is little left over to sell. Jigawa has a hot, dry **windswept climate**. Without refrigeration, it is hard for farmers to **preserve** food.

Bacteria can **spoil** food quickly in hot weather. Eating spoiled food can make people sick. It also causes problems for farmers.

MOHAMMED BAH ABBA

Mohammed Bah Abba is a teacher from Jigawa. He saw the problems the farmers had. They needed to sell extra **produce** quickly before it spoiled. The farmers' children, especially girls, skipped school to sell the families' produce.

Abba wanted to help the farmers. His family's skill was making **ceramic** pots. He thought of a way to preserve food using these pots. He called his invention a pot-in-pot.

First, Abba put a small pot inside a big pot. Then he put wet sand between the two pots. Next, he put vegetables inside the smaller pot. The water in the sand began to **evaporate**, or change from a liquid to a gas. This took heat away from the smaller pot, keeping the vegetables cool. Food can stay fresh for almost two weeks in a pot-in-pot.

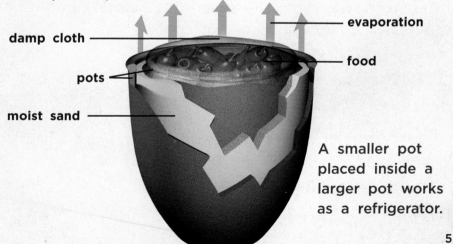

damp cloth

evaporation

pots

food

moist sand

A smaller pot placed inside a larger pot works as a refrigerator.

A NOT-SO-ORDINARY POT

Abba's community made his idea a success. There were many pot makers in Jigawa. There were also many people who needed jobs. These people got jobs making or selling the pot-in-pots.

The community also helped in other ways. Some people gave Abba a place to work. Others helped him deliver the pot-in-pots to the people who bought them.

EVAPORATIVE COOLERS

When water gets hot, it evaporates. It turns from a liquid into a gas. The gas is called *water vapor*.

In a pot-in-pot, the outside pot gets hot and heats up the wet sand. The heat makes water vapor move out of the sand between the pots. The vapor takes heat away from the sand. This helps keep vegetables inside the inner pot cool.

STOP AND CHECK

Why did Mohammed Bah Abba invent the pot-in-pot?

Abba's idea has improved the lives of the people of Jigawa.

The pot-in-pot keeps food fresh. Farmers have more time to sell their produce. They do not need to go to the market every day.

The pot-in-pot also helps farmers make more money. They no longer have to sell their food quickly and cheaply before it spoils. Instead, they can charge a fair price.

Mohammed Bah Abba explains how to make the pot-in-pot.

COMMUNITY BENEFITS

The pot-in-pot helps people stay healthy by keeping their food cool and fresh. This also helps them save money. Healthy people spend less money on doctors and have more time to farm.

Education is expensive in Nigeria. Often only boys go to school. With the pot-in-pot, some families might be able to send all of their children to school.

Farmers using pot-in-pots do not have to rush to sell their produce.

BEYOND JIGAWA

The pot-in-pot only works in a hot, dry climate. Many rural villages in Africa are **arid**. A pot-in-pot can keep food cool and safe in these villages.

Pot-in-pots began in Nigeria. Now people use them in African countries both near and far from Nigeria.

This woman is cooking yams and sweet potatoes. These are common foods in Nigeria.

STOP AND CHECK

How has the pot-in-pot helped people?

CHAPTER 2
A NEW IDEA FOR PARAGUAY

The people of Caaguazú (*kah-ah-gwah-SEW*) in Paraguay are subsistence farmers, like the people in Jigawa. Some farmers are **sharecroppers**. They rent land and pay for it with part of their crops. Other farmers use a **traditional** system from their past called *minga*. People work on each other's farms during busy times. Like children in Jigawa, children in Caaguazú often work instead of going to school.

Soy is one of the main crops in Paraguay.

Most farmers in Caaguazú used to plant cotton. Then the price of soybeans tripled. So, many farmers switched to planting soy.

Planting soy caused problems for the farmers. The soybean crops damaged the soil. Farmers couldn't grow other crops. This caused the farms' **productivity** to fall, or **decline**. Many families could not grow enough food. They had to leave their farms.

ELSA ZALDÍVAR

Elsa Zaldívar is a community worker in Caaguazú. She wanted to help the local people improve their lives. She thought that the best way to do this was to help women make money.

Zaldívar noticed a vegetable called loofah. It is **abundant** in Caaguazú. She wondered if this plant could help create jobs for women.

Loofah can be eaten as a vegetable. It can also be dried and used as a sponge. Zaldívar thought that other uses could be **unearthed**.

Dried loofah can be used as a skin scrubber.

LOOFAH CREATES JOBS

First, Zaldívar talked to local women who wanted to earn money. Then the women worked with her to grow loofah and find ways to use it.

Loofah grows on vines.

After many tries, the women discovered what they could make with loofah. They made products such as mats, slippers, and insoles for shoes. Finally, they sold their goods to markets in other places **overseas**, such as Europe and China.

Making these products used only a third of the loofah plant. The women threw the rest away. Zaldívar didn't like wasting any of the loofah. She soon found a new way to use the rest of it.

STOP AND CHECK

What are some ways to use loofah?

LOOFAH HOUSES

The people of Caaguazú needed cheaper and more **affordable** houses. Zaldívar worked with an engineer named Pedro Padrós to make house panels from loofah. Padrós invented a machine to make these panels. The loofah in the panels acted as insulation. It kept the houses warm.

Women collected the leftover loofah and gave it to Padrós. Other people brought leftover plastic, which was also needed for the panels. **Recycling** the plastic was good for the environment.

COMBINING PLASTIC WITH VEGETABLES

To make housing panels, Padrós and Zaldívar mixed loofah, corn husks, and palm husks. They added the plant mixture to recycled plastic. The plastic works like glue. It holds everything together. The panels can be used more than once. Old panels can be melted down and made into new panels.

A worker makes panels with the machine invented by Padrós.

COMMUNITY CHANGE

The local women grew loofah and sold their products. Their new businesses created jobs for people in their community.

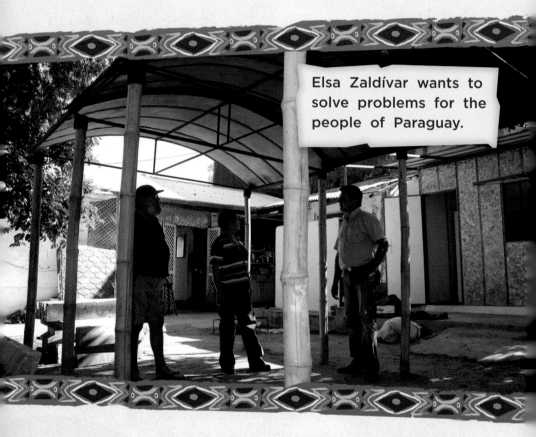

Elsa Zaldívar wants to solve problems for the people of Paraguay.

Zaldívar's idea gave women a way to earn money. Because the women earn more, their children can go to school instead of working.

Many children in Paraguay now go to school instead of working on farms.

People use the housing panels to make affordable homes. They can even build their own houses. This means they don't have to pay a builder.

Many people worked together to make these houses possible. Sharing ideas has led to positive changes in their lives.

STOP AND CHECK

How do the housing panels help people?

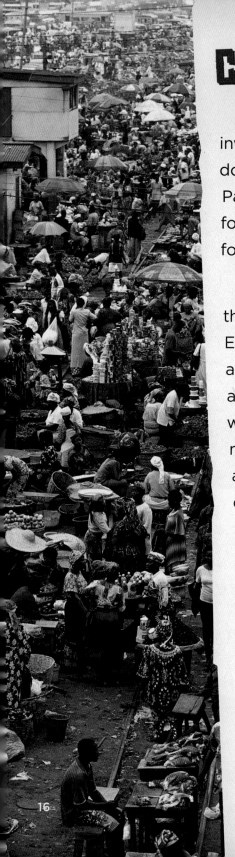

CONCLUSION

In Nigeria, a teacher invented a refrigerator that doesn't need electricity. In Paraguay, a community worker found a way to create jobs for women.

Abba and Zaldívar shared their ideas with other people. Everyone worked together and learned from one another. Abba and Zaldivar worked with local people and materials. They both made a big difference in their communities.

The market is a center of community life in Nigeria.

Abba's and Zaldívar's ideas mean that more children can go to school. Education will give these children more choices in the future. Their lives will be improved. Over time, so will the lives of their families and their communities.

Many Nigerian girls no longer have to sell vegetables during the school day.

Summarize

Use important details from *Coming Together for Change.* Summarize how people helped their communities. Your graphic organizer may help you.

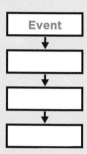

Event

Text Evidence

1. In Chapter 2, what events helped people use loofah to improve their lives? SEQUENCE

2. Find the word *backgrounds* on page 3. What clues help you to figure out the word's meaning? VOCABULARY

3. How did the pot-in-pot come to be used in Mohammed Bah Abba's community? Write about the events in order. WRITE ABOUT READING

Compare Texts
Read about how students worked
together to help people.

Food for Thought

Characters:

ANNA **MARA** **BEN** **ELIZABETH** **ZACHARY**

Scene: *A classroom*
School has finished for the day. **ANNA**, **MARA**,
BEN, **ELIZABETH**, *and* **ZACHARY** *are meeting.*

ANNA: Thanks for coming, everyone. Mrs. Collins
wants an idea for a project to help people. Does
anyone have any ideas?

MARA: How about a comedy night? I've been practicing
my jokes.

ANNA: Um...does anyone else have an idea?

ZACHARY: What about the homeless shelter?

BEN: Or maybe the food bank or community center.

ELIZABETH: Those are all good ideas. How can we
choose the best one?

MARA: Let's pick one idea out of a hat. That's how my mom decides everything.

ZACHARY: I like Ben's idea of the food bank.

Everyone nods and murmurs.

ANNA: Raise your hand if you think helping the food bank is a good idea.

ELIZABETH, **ANNA**, **BEN**, *and* **ZACHARY** *raise their hands.* **MARA** *does not.*

MARA: So no one wants to put on a comedy night?

ANNA: Maybe next time, Mara. Okay, let's figure out the details. Ben, will you talk to the people who run the food bank?

BEN *nods and writes in his notebook.*

ANNA: And Elizabeth, would you make fliers? Mara can draw something to show what we're collecting.

ZACHARY: Cans and boxes are probably best. That kind of food lasts longest.

BEN: There's a bulletin board at the library. I bet they'll let us put up a flier.

ELIZABETH: (*holding up a sheet of paper*) What do you think of this? It shows when and where to drop off food.

Two weeks later, the students are gathered around a large collection of boxes and cans.

ELIZABETH: What a mountain of food!

ANNA: It's awesome! Lots of people wanted to help.

ZACHARY: We should do a food drive every year.

ELIZABETH: Good idea, Zachary. We can help lots of people that way!

ANNA: I'll talk to Mrs. Collins about it. I'm sure she'll agree.

BEN: Maybe we could collect books for the library.

MARA: I still think we should have a comedy night.

ANNA: (*shaking her head*) Maybe in the spring.

MARA: (*pumping her fist in the air*) Yes!

Make Connections

How do Anna and her friends decide on an idea for their project? ESSENTIAL QUESTION

How do people work together in *Coming Together for Change* and *Food for Thought*?
TEXT TO TEXT

Glossary

arid *(A-ruhd)* very dry *(page 9)*

ceramic *(suh-RA-mik)* made from clay or earth and heated to high temperatures *(page 5)*

climate *(KLIGH-muht)* type of weather *(page 4)*

evaporate *(i-VAP-uh-rayt)* to turn from a liquid into a gas *(page 5)*

preserve *(pri-ZURV)* store something in a way that prevents it from decaying or decomposing *(page 4)*

produce *(PRO-dews)* things that have been produced or grown, such as fruits, vegetables, and grains *(page 5)*

recycling *(ree-SIGH-kling)* reusing something, either in its original form or by making it into something new *(page 13)*

refrigeration *(ri-fri-juh-RAY-shuhn)* the process of cooling or freezing *(page 4)*

spoil *(spoyl)* lose freshness or nutritional value *(page 4)*

subsistence *(suhb-SIS-tuhns)* having only enough to stay alive *(page 4)*

Index

Focus on Social Studies

Purpose To understand the benefits of working as a group

What to Do

Step 1 Plan a project like the one that Anna and the other students did in *Food for Thought*. List projects that could help people.

Step 2 First, work on your own. Think about how you would raise money or help one of your projects. Make a list of what you need for your plan.

Step 3 Next, work with a partner. Talk about each other's plans. Write down the best ideas and make a new plan.

Step 4 Talk about what you have done. Was it easier working by yourself or with a partner? Explain why.